FORGED ON FREEDOM
THE MAKING OF AMERICA

The
AMENDMENTS
to the Constitution

Tamra Orr

PURPLE TOAD
PUBLISHING

P.O. Box 631
Kennett Square, Pennsylvania 19348
www.purpletoadpublishing.com

FORGED ON FREEDOM

THE MAKING OF AMERICA

The Constitution: Defender of Freedom
The Amendments to the Constitution
The Revolutionary War: The War for Freedom
Roots of the Revolution

Copyright © 2014 by Purple Toad Publishing, Inc.

Printing 1 2 3 4 5 6 7 8 9

Publisher's Cataloging-in-Publication Data
Orr, Tamra
    The Amendments to the constitution / Tamra Orr
        p. cm.—(Forged on freedom)
Includes bibliographic references and index.
ISBN: 978-1-62469-070-9 (library bound)
1. Constitutional amendments. 2. United States.
Constitution—Juvenile literature.   I. Title.
 K3168 2013
  342.03—dc23
                                                        2013946328

eBook ISBN: 9781624690716

Printed by Lake Book Manufacturing, Chicago, IL

CONTENTS

Lincoln's Inner
BATTLE

President Abraham Lincoln sat quietly at the empty table. The room was silent, but his mind was teeming with a passionate jumble of emotions and words. He hung his head, as if the noise inside made it too heavy for him to hold it up any longer. He felt like the fate of the world truly weighed upon his shoulders. Countless people were looking to him for wise leadership and decision making. Others were hoping he would just give up the fight. Everyone knew that whatever he decided would determine their futures, for better or worse.

Lincoln had no doubt in his mind that slavery was wrong. It was morally wrong. It was legally wrong. He knew he had to end it, but he didn't know how to without betraying the country's Constitution. How could he put an end to a practice he knew was wrong when the nation's highest law said it was right?

Lincoln felt his shoulders slump farther as the burden of this immense decision circled in his mind. Freeing the slaves might be the right goal, but how would he ever be able to accomplish it, and would the country survive the war it would certainly ignite?

Lincoln remains one of the most beloved historical figures in America and has been continually voted the most influential president in the country's long history.

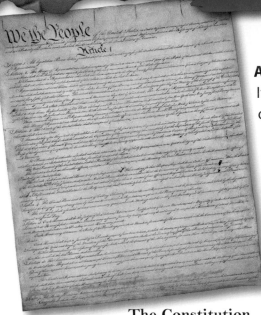

The Constitution

A New Point of View

It's easy to glance at a history textbook, or a copy of the U.S. Constitution, and see nothing but a list of numbers and a style of writing that seems confusing and complicated. However, history is actually made up of people, decisions, and struggle, not numbers and years.

For example, as you read through the 13th Amendment, you may not recognize the turmoil behind it. You might see some words about slavery, but may not realize that behind those words was a desperate and determined president, and a country at war—plus frustrated and concerned plantation owners, tired soldiers, and an entire race of people longing for the most basic of human rights—freedom.

The amendments may seem dull, but remember that each one was weighed and considered by people with worries, fears, and hopes for a better world. Each one of these amendments was written, proposed, debated, voted on, and eventually passed in order to make the United States a safer, and more just country. The 27 amendments to this nation's Constitution are in place because of leaders like President Lincoln who sat alone and did everything he could to find a solution that would strengthen the country and its people.

Then—Yes! Now?

Reading words that were put into place more than 200 years ago may make you ask how they could possibly be relevant today. Life was much different then than it is now. How could the concerns and issues of the late 18th century possibly relate to the ones of the early 21st?

While the world has changed in many ways in the past two centuries, some elements have stayed the same. The need for justice, privacy, and

Benjamin Franklin (left), John Adams (seated), and Thomas Jefferson (standing) were part of the main group of founding fathers which also included Alexander Hamilton, John Jay, James Madison, and George Washington.

freedom are the same for you as they were for the Founding Fathers. The rights these men wrote about in the Bill of Rights are no different than the ones you expect today. You want the freedom to be a Protestant, while your friend may want the same right to be a Mormon, Catholic, Pagan, Muslim, or atheist. You want the right to speak, read, or write your opinions without worrying that the government will censor them. Certainly, if you run into trouble, you want the right to post a reasonable bail, receive a fair and speedy trial, and not have to worry about being tortured while you are detained.

The men who labored to create the country's Constitution were very wise in a number of ways. They knew that, as the decades passed, the country would continue to change, especially in ways they could not possibly imagine. In order to adapt to these changes and create a document that would "endure for ages,"[1] as Supreme Court Justice John

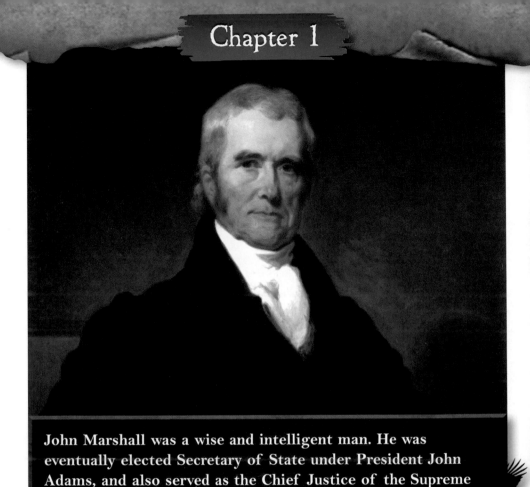

John Marshall was a wise and intelligent man. He was eventually elected Secretary of State under President John Adams, and also served as the Chief Justice of the Supreme Court.

Marshall once stated, it had to be possible to amend the Constitution. Those changes, or amendments, would reflect the issues of the time.

The inclusion of the amendment process of the Constitution shows incredible foresight on the part of the men who wrote it. Although clever, it is a long, detailed, and challenging task. The Founding Fathers found this out the hard way, too. They were assigned the job of writing those first amendments—the Bill of Rights.

Spielberg's *Lincoln*

In 2012, Steven Spielberg's epic film *Lincoln* was released in theaters across the country. Abraham Lincoln was played by actor Daniel Day-Lewis. His wife, Mary, was portrayed by Sally Field. The movie centered on the president's last few months in the White House and his passionate and powerful battle to abolish slavery throughout the United States. The movie was a tremendous hit, bringing in large audiences of all ages and earning Day-Lewis an Oscar for Best Actor.[2]

We, The People

Although the Bill of Rights is considered one of the most important documents written in U.S. history, there are many Americans who have little-to-no idea what it says. A recent survey showed that one in three people polled could identify the Bill of Rights. Not even one person in ten knew why it had been written and passed in the first place. Twenty-eight percent of the people thought that the Bill of Rights was the Preamble to the Constitution and seven percent of the people confused it with the Declaration of Independence.

You don't want to be one of these statistics! Read on and see how Lincoln used the Bill of Rights to end slavery.

Daniel Day-Lewis
as Lincoln

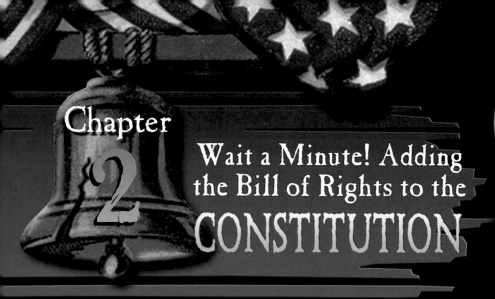

Chapter 2

Wait a Minute! Adding the Bill of Rights to the CONSTITUTION

Although the Constitution was passed in 1776, not everyone was pleased with how it turned out. A number of delegates were worried about the lack of what they called a "bill of rights" or a clear list of which rights and liberties were allowed for each person. These men were called Anti-Federalists.[1]

Their concern was understandable. They had just spent years battling for freedom and independence, and they wanted to make sure they would keep them. Representatives from some states objected to a constitution that did not clearly state that citizens had freedom of speech and religion, or failed to put enough limits on the government. Delegates from other states argued that no extra rules were needed. Everything was implied in the Constitution already. These men were called Federalists.[2]

In the end, the Anti-Federalists' opinion won. Enough people were worried that their rights were not going to be protected enough that the representatives all agreed to add a list of rights to the country's brand new constitution.

The ongoing battle between the Federalists and Anti-Federalists often appeared in newspaper editorials, letters, and even political cartoons such as this one from 1787.

Drafting the Bill of Rights took time, dedication, hard work, and an endless number of debates and discussions. Many amendments were considered, analyzed, revised, and then either accepted or rejected. When it was finally sent to the states for ratification, the Bill of Rights was made up of twelve amendments. Two were never ratified. The remaining ten comprise the current version of the document.[3]

The Process of Ratification

Getting a Constitution or even an amendment ratified is a very complex and time-consuming process. To better understand it, imagine that you want to officially change one of the rules in your household. Perhaps you want to stay up later, get more time on the computer, increase your allowance, or only do chores on the weekends.

For this example, let's imagine you want to get a part time job, even though in your house, the rule is no working until your senior year of high school. You write up a formal document proposing the idea, making sure to include up-to-date details and persuasive arguments that prove the validity of your request.

You propose the idea to your parents. They discuss it, and then you and your parents start negotiating the terms of the amendment to the house rules. You want a part-time job to make some money. They worry that you will spend as much time and money getting to your job as you will earn. You point out that you can bike to the job, and they say it depends on where you work. The three of you go back and forth, stating opinions, sharing concerns, and finally reaching an agreement.

This is what happens when a member of Congress proposes an amendment. That is when the ratification process begins. The amendment is either taken to a convention of representatives where people discuss and eventually vote, or it is sent out for popular vote to each state. In your example, now that you and your parents have agreed on the basic terms, your suggestion will be sent out for voting from other involved parties.

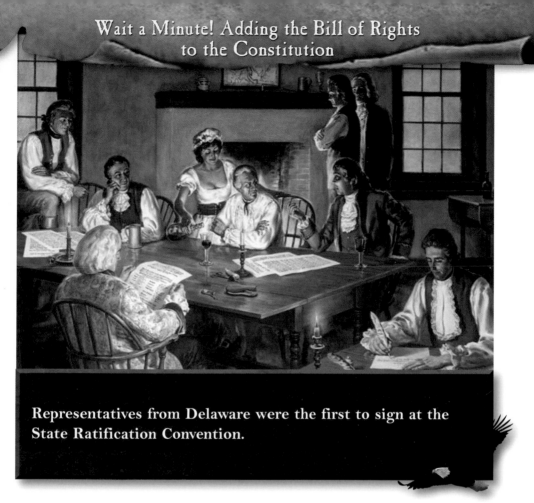

Representatives from Delaware were the first to sign at the State Ratification Convention.

Will your teachers agree with the terms? Your coach? Your friends? Your grandparents? Your neighbors? Each one of these people may have a real interest in whether or not you get a part-time job. Your teachers may say no because they are worried about how the addition of a job to your daily schedule will affect your grades. Your track coach may suspect you will stop practicing as much if you're working—or even quit the team altogether. Your friends may not like the idea because it means you will have less time to hang out with them. Your grandparents love you, so they might just agree with you for that reason alone. Your neighbors may like the idea because you won't be playing your music as loudly in the middle of the afternoon. If each one of these people is allowed to vote on your idea, you may not end up getting what you want—and your idea/amendment will not be accepted/ratified. You will be back where you started, despite your time, hard work, and effort.

This is what happens during the ratification process except, instead of asking a dozen or so people to give their opinions, amendments are debated by hundreds of people, each with his or her own personal concerns and questions. It is little wonder that it took more than two years between drafting the Bill of Rights and having it ratified by at least three-fourths of the states.[4]

Understanding the Bill of Rights

The Bill of Rights is a set of ten liberties the country's Founding Fathers thought were the most important to have in writing.

When the Founding Fathers developed these rights, they argued, debated, and bickered. Although they all had different ideas of what belonged on the list, or how each amendment should be phrased, they agreed on one thing—they did not want their new country to be governed like England. Their battle to protect the people's rights stemmed from the unfair treatment they had escaped from after the Revolutionary War. It was the fuel igniting their passion to create a better country than the one they had left behind. Let's take a look at each one of the rights. What is in the Bill of Rights? Here is a detailed list. All were ratified at once on December 15, 1791.[5]

The Beginning of the Bill of Rights

Wait a Minute! Adding the Bill of Rights to the Constitution

Amendment	As Written	Meaning
I	Congress shall make no law respecting an establishment of religion, or prohibiting the free exercise thereof; or abridging the freedom of speech, or of the press; or the right of the people peaceably to assemble, and to petition the Government for a redress of grievances.	This amendment focuses on individual freedoms, including freedom of religion, speech/expression, and assembly. This means you can gather and meet (although you need a permit), say what you want about government leaders (although libel and slander are not allowed), and attend whatever church—or none—that you prefer. If you have ever heard the expression of "separation of church and state," this is the amendment that created it. It means that no government (or school or business) can tell you what religion to follow.
II	A well regulated Militia, being necessary to the security of a free State, the right of the people to keep and bear Arms, shall not be infringed.	This is the amendment that is most often quoted by people who want to own guns. The 2nd Amendment is what gives them the right, although state and federal gun laws regulate the sale, possession, and use of firearms.
III	No Soldier shall, in time of peace be quartered in any house, without the consent of the Owner, nor in time of war, but in a manner to be prescribed by law.	This amendment protects citizens from having to share their homes with soldiers during wartime or in time of peace.
IV	The right of the people to be secure in their persons, houses, papers, and effects, against unreasonable searches and seizures, shall not be violated, and no Warrants shall issue, but upon probable cause, supported by Oath or affirmation, and particularly describing the place to be searched, and the persons or things to be seized.	This amendment is commonly considered the one affecting personal privacy. It is what makes it illegal to search a person's home, papers, and belongings without a warrant. This special document must detail exactly what is being searched for and why and has to be signed by a judge.
V	No person shall be held to answer for a capital, or otherwise infamous crime, unless on a presentment or indictment of a Grand Jury, except in cases arising in the land or naval forces, or in the Militia, when in actual service in time of War or public danger; nor shall any person be subject for the same offence to be twice put in jeopardy of life or limb; nor shall be compelled in any criminal case to be a witness against himself, nor be deprived of life, liberty, or property, without due process of law; nor shall private property be taken for public use, without just compensation.	This amendment protects people involved in criminal cases and is often referred to as the "due process of law." The 5th Amendment includes several important rights including not being forced to testify against yourself in court, not being tried for the same crime more than once, and not being taken to court unless it has been determined a crime has been committed. This amendment also explains the term "eminent domain," or the concept that your private property cannot be taken unless you are fairly paid for it.

VI	In all criminal prosecutions, the accused shall enjoy the right to a speedy and public trial, by an impartial jury of the State and district wherein the crime shall have been committed, which district shall have been previously ascertained by law, and to be informed of the nature and cause of the accusation; to be confronted with the witnesses against him; to have compulsory process for obtaining witnesses in his favor, and to have the Assistance of Counsel for his defence.	This is the amendment making sure that if you are arrested you will get a quick and fair trial by a jury of your equals or peers. You will be told what crime you committed, why you have been arrested, and when to get a lawyer and witnesses ready.
VII	In Suits at common law, where the value in controversy shall exceed twenty dollars, the right of trial by jury shall be preserved, and no fact tried by a jury, shall be otherwise re-examined in any Court of the United States, than according to the rules of the common law.	This amendment is about lawsuits and lets you know that if you are arrested in a civil suit that will be heard in federal court, you have the right to a jury trial, just as you do in a criminal trial.
VIII	Excessive bail shall not be required, nor excessive fines imposed, nor cruel and unusual punishments inflicted.	This amendment is for those who have been arrested and detained. The rule states that the bail set will be in proportion to the crime itself (a reasonable amount of money that will be returned if you appear in court when directed), and that cruel and unusual punishment is not allowed.
IX	The enumeration in the Constitution, of certain rights, shall not be construed to deny or disparage others retained by the people.	This amendment continues to puzzle historians and other experts. It states that the naming of certain rights within the Constitution does not mean that other rights that were NOT named have been taken away. However, it provides no clues to what those rights might be.
X	The powers not delegated to the United States by the Constitution, nor prohibited by it to the States, are reserved to the States respectively, or to the people.	This amendment means that the Constitution gives the federal government specific powers, gives the state governments specific powers, and gives the people specific powers.

Alexander Hamilton was a Federalist, and he believed the federal government's power should be limited and that no other rules were needed. He asked, "Why declare that things shall not be done which there is no power to do? Why, for instance, should it be said that the liberty of the press shall not be restrained, when no power is given by which restrictions may be imposed?"[7]

In addition to being a Federalist, Hamilton helped establish the country's first national bank, and founded a daily paper that remains in print today— *The New York Post.*

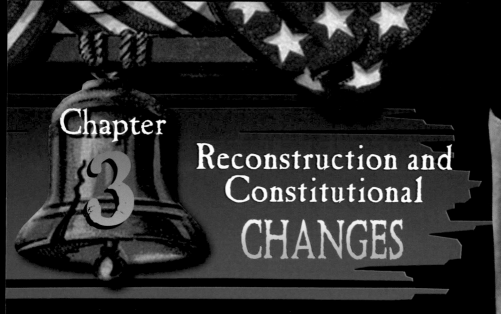

Chapter 3

Reconstruction and Constitutional CHANGES

Coming up with an idea for an amendment and proposing it is fairly simple. Getting it passed, however, is altogether different. As you have learned, the ratification process is both slow and complex.

For four years after the Bill of Rights was accepted, no other amendment made it through the rigorous process of being ratified. Finally, in 1795, the 11th Amendment was passed.[1] It read,

> *"The Judicial power of the United States shall not be construed to extend to any suit in law or Equity, commenced or prosecuted against one of the United States by Citizens of another State, or by Citizens or Subjects of any Foreign State."*[2]

Essentially, this amendment detailed what type of lawsuit the federal government would listen to and which it would not.

The 12th Amendment was not added to the Constitution for another nine years. In June 1804,

The passage of the 13th Amendment drastically changed the country as people were strongly divided on the abolishment of slavery.

The election of 1804 was the first one to fall under the ruling of the 12th Amendment. Thomas Jefferson was elected president and George Clinton became vice president.

it was passed.[3] It revised the procedure for electing the country's president and vice president. The procedure that had been used up until then, based on the Electoral College, had resulted in enough complications that it became clear changes were needed. This very long and detailed amendment impacted elections in several ways, including putting the president and vice president together on the same ballot. Prior to this amendment, representatives voted for one of several candidates for president. The one who received the most votes became president. The one who was second runner-up was the new vice president. If people from different parties or with extremely opposing opinions were elected, it could cause big problems. They might struggle to work as a team, plus, if the president died, and the vice president took over, it could drastically change the political balance of power.[4]

The Reconstruction Amendments

Of all the amendments that were passed after the Bill of Rights, the 13th was one of the most profound in that it affected many people's lives in many ways. The amendment itself was brief and to the point.

"Neither slavery nor involuntary servitude, except as punishment for crime whereof the party shall have been duly convicted, shall exist within the United States, or any place subject to their jurisdiction. Congress shall have power to enforce this article by appropriate legislation."[5]

When the 13th Amendment was passed at the end of 1865, it had been over 60 years since the last one had been adopted. The 13th was the first of the three Reconstruction Amendments, as they were known. Lincoln used the term "reconstruction" in one of his speeches. He had hoped that the country would be rebuilt from "half slave and half free"[6] to one that was more equal for all males.

The 13th Amendment was a natural follow-up to Lincoln's Emancipation Proclamation, issued in 1863.[7] This proclamation was an executive order that came out during the Civil War. While this order freed the majority of slaves, it did not cover the 800,000 living in Union states on the border between the north and south, such as Missouri, Kentucky, West Virginia, Maryland, and Delaware.[8]

While the Emancipation Proclamation and the 13th Amendment did a great deal to help free the slaves, they did not solve all of the problems. More was needed. The 14th Amendment was the second of the reconstruction amendments. It was adopted in summer of 1868, and focused on which people qualified as citizens, including African Americans. This idea was in direct opposition of the court decision that had been handed down in 1857. Known as the Dred Scott case, the

Dred Scott's trial went on for more than a decade and finally ended up in the Supreme Court which ruled that all people of African ancestry would never be citizens and could not sue in federal court.

court ruled that blacks held as slaves, as well as their descendants, were not and never would be citizens. Therefore, their rights were not protected under the Constitution.[9] The 14th Amendment was adopted to give blacks full citizenship. This was hard for some of the Southern states to accept.

The third reconstruction amendment was passed in 1870. Now that blacks had been freed and guaranteed protection under the Constitution as equal citizens, it was time to make sure they were also allowed to vote in elections.

The 15th Amendment states,

"The right of citizens of the United States to vote shall not be denied or abridged by the United States or by any State on account of race, color, or previous condition of servitude. The Congress shall have power to enforce this article by appropriate legislation."[10]

That same year an African American man named Thomas Mundy Peterson was the first black person to cast a ballot in a New Jersey schoolboard election. Although blacks were finally able to vote, women

Elizabeth Cady Stanton fought hard and long to gain the right to vote. She is famous for her speech "Declaration of Sentiments," delivered at the first women's rights convention held in Seneca, New York, in 1848.

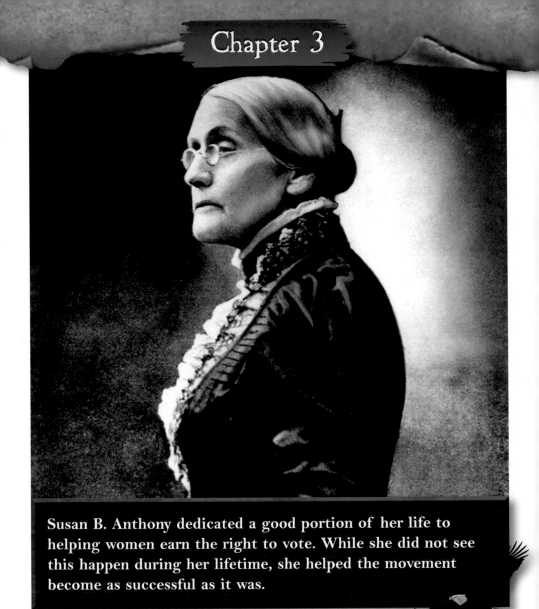

Susan B. Anthony dedicated a good portion of her life to helping women earn the right to vote. While she did not see this happen during her lifetime, she helped the movement become as successful as it was.

were still left out. Many suffragettes, such as Elizabeth Cady Stanton and Susan B. Anthony, campaigned hard and long to help blacks earn the right to vote. Once that happened, unfortunately, the fight for their own right to vote was dropped for many years.[11]

The Civil War brought many changes to the country, and those changes were largely reflected in the three reconstruction amendments passed in the years right after the war. These new national rules were the last ones made in the 19th century. Which new changes would be made in the new century?

Susan B. Anthony and Slavery

Although Susan B. Anthony is best known for her work to earn women the right to vote, she was also a champion of abolition, or the fight against slavery. When the Civil War began, Anthony shifted her focus to ending slavery. She, along with the Women's National Loyal League, circulated petitions to speed up the passage of the 13th Amendment.[12]

The Women's National Loyal League was organized by the powerhouse duo of Stanton and Anthony, two women who had no trouble standing up for what they believed in.

Chapter 4

A New Century BEGINS

As the 19th century came to an end, and the 20th century began, the North and South were no longer bitterly divided as they had been a few decades before. The world was changing rapidly. In 1901, the first radio transmission was sent across the Atlantic Ocean. A couple of years later, brothers Orville and Wilbur Wright had discovered the mystery of flight. In 1908, Henry T. Ford had found a way to make his Model T cars on an assembly line.

The first amendment to be passed in the new century was one relating to income taxes, and is known as the Revenue Act of 1913. Before this amendment, income taxes were collected in several different ways. During the Civil War, the government put a three percent tax on incomes in order to raise money for supplies. Other times, taxes were determined based on state populations.[1]

The 20th century was a time of major change and progress, including the first chance for humans to leave the earth and explore the sky.

The 16th Amendment reads,

"The Congress shall have power to lay and collect taxes on incomes from whatever source derived, without apportionment among the several States and without regard to any census or enumeration."[2]

The 16th Amendment certainly plays a role in people's lives today, especially in April of each year when federal income taxes must be paid to the government. These taxes are based on many factors, including annual income. Like a century ago, the money is used to pay for the country's government programs and services.

The 17th Amendment is another one that focuses on the election process.[3]

If you look over all 27 amendments, it may seem that a great deal of time and effort was spent on detailing just how government leaders can be elected and how long they can serve. This is a high priority for legislators. This is because many of the lawmakers remember how the Founding Fathers struggled to make sure America would never have the tyrannical leadership it once had under British rule.

The focus of this amendment, passed in 1913, was on the process of electing U.S. senators.[4] Prior to this, senators were elected by state legislatures. With the passing of the 17th Amendment, however, senators would be elected by popular vote and would serve a term of six years.

Prohibition: Here and Gone
The story surrounding the 18th Amendment is a unique one. In the long history of the Constitution, only one amendment has been passed and then required another amendment to reverse it. The idea started in the 1800s, and was based on a movement, largely led by Christian women, called temperance.[5] Believing that the use of alcohol resulted in everything from violent crime and poverty to immorality and poor health, these women wanted to ban alcohol from the entire country.

Under the watchful eyes of the police, saloon keepers pour their supply of illegal alcohol into the local sewer.

The 18th Amendment made it illegal to make, sell, or transport beer, wine, or liquor of any kind. It was passed in 1919, but did not take effect until early 1920. Known as "the noble experiment,"[6] Prohibition truly did change the country although not necessarily in the ways many had hoped. Restaurants and theaters closed due to lack of business. Unemployment soared as the thousands of people who worked in breweries, distilleries, and saloons were out of work. The taxes that had been applied to alcohol sales disappeared, impacting state budgets.[7]

Although alcohol was not available in the usual places, it was still available. Pharmacists could dispense whiskey as a treatment for anything from stress to insomnia. Attendance at churches and temples

Winston Churchill once said, "History is written by the victors," and though prohibition is looked down upon today by the masses, many believe that had people obeyed its laws, thousands of lives would've been saved from deaths attributed to drunk driving and alcohol-related violence.

soared because wine was allowed for religious ceremonies. People began brewing their own liquor at home and called it "moonshine." Many Americans died because of drinking alcohol that had been made incorrectly.[8]

Worst of all, Prohibition devastated the justice system. Many police officers gave in to bribes to look the other way. Millions of people got involved in the illegal liquor trade, and the following arrests flooded the courts and jails. Crime bosses organized groups of criminals which increased criminal activity from mobs like the Mafia.[9] Some people spent a year in jail waiting for a trial.

Prohibition was a failure in that it did not stop the sale or use of alcohol, and it created problems for the country in other ways. It would take 14 years, but this amendment would finally be repealed.[10] Will Rogers, a man known for his sharp wit and sense of humor, once stated, "Instead of giving money to found colleges to promote learning, why don't we pass a constitutional amendment prohibiting anybody from learning anything? If it works as good as the Prohibition one did, why, in five years, we would have the smartest race of people on earth."[11]

The Women's Turn, At Last!

For decades, women had been campaigning for the right to vote, and had been turned down. During the Civil War, they fought hard to earn the freedom of slaves and the right to vote for African American men as well as liberties for themselves. When the 13th Amendment passed, suffragettes were sure they were next—but they weren't. It took until the 19th Amendment, passed in 1920, for women to finally be allowed to vote.[12] Sadly, this came 14 years after the death of Susan B. Anthony, the woman who is known for leading the movement.

Suffragettes celebrate the passing of the 19th Amendment.

Women fought hard for the right to vote.

The 19th Amendment's wording is simple and straightforward.

"The right of citizens of the United States to vote shall not be denied or abridged by the United States or by any State on account of sex. Congress shall have power to enforce this article by appropriate legislation."[13]

The next amendment focused, once again, on determining the correct election process for the United States. Ratified in 1933, the 20th Amendment established the beginning and end of the terms of various elected officials, as well as what should be done if there is no president-elect.[14] According to this amendment, the terms of the president and vice president end at noon on January 20, while senators' and representatives' terms end on January 3. If, for some reason, there is no president, the vice president will take his or her place.

That same year, the 21st Amendment was passed, putting an end to the era of Prohibition. It was the only amendment in U.S. history to be decided through state ratifying conventions, rather than through votes in state legislatures. The amendment took effect ten days before Christmas 1933.[15]

The first half of the new century witnessed the passing of six amendments that drastically changed the lives of Americans. By 1950, women were voting, alcohol was back on the market, and election processes were better defined. The rest of the century would be spent further clarifying how the election process works in America—a decision the Founding Fathers would most likely have approved.

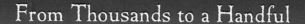

From Thousands to a Handful

Since 1789, more than 10,000 proposals for amendments have been made. Only a tiny fraction of those ideas receive enough support to go through the constitutional ratification process. In fact, the success rate for a proposed amendment to actually become part of the Constitution is less than one percent. About 500 of these proposals focus on changing the presidential election process.[16]

People continue to propose constitutional amendments in an ongoing effort to refine the rules that govern the United States.

Chapter 5

Ongoing Changes: Amendments of the Past 50 YEARS

Has the Constitution been amended often in the last half century? Between 1951 and 1992, there have been six amendments passed. All of them have focused on election processes in one way or another.

For many years, none of the amendments that were proposed were passed. That changed in 1951 when the 22nd Amendment was adopted. It took almost four years for it to be ratified and it stated that the president of the United States can only serve a total of two consecutive terms.[1] Until this passed, a number of men had served two terms or more. Some of them served the remaining term of presidents who had died or been assassinated. To date, the presidents who served two consecutive terms include

- George Washington
- Thomas Jefferson
- James Madison
- James Monroe
- Andrew Jackson
- Ulysses S. Grant

- Woodrow Wilson
- Dwight D. Eisenhower
- Ronald Reagan
- Bill Clinton
- George W. Bush[2]

Franklin D. Roosevelt was one of America's favorite presidents and served longer than any other leader in the country's history.

Franklin D. Roosevelt served three terms and was elected for a fourth, but died while in office.[3] Because of his re-election in November 2012, Barack Obama will most likely be added to this list.

The 23rd Amendment was a very specific one, giving the people living in the District of Columbia the right to vote in presidential elections. Prior to ratification in 1961, these residents were not permitted to vote because Washington, D.C., is not a state.[4]

Only three years passed before the 24th Amendment was added to the Constitution. Proposed in 1962, it was adopted in 1964. The text reads,

Even though Washington, D.C., is the nation's capital and the seat of the White House, its people only recently gained the right to vote in the last 50 years.

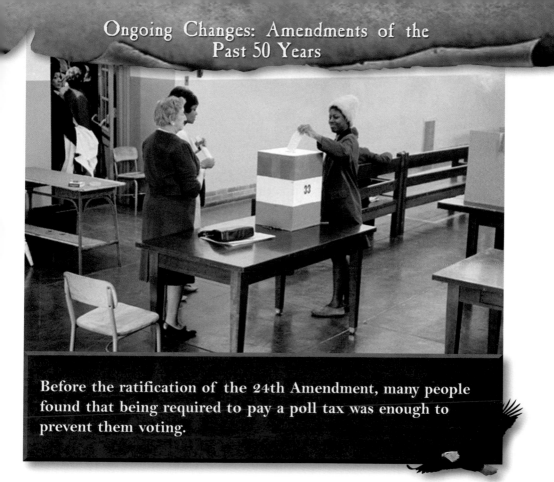

Before the ratification of the 24th Amendment, many people found that being required to pay a poll tax was enough to prevent them voting.

"The right of citizens of the United States to vote in any primary or other election for President or Vice President, for electors for President or Vice President, or for Senator or Representative in Congress, shall not be denied or abridged by the United States or any State by reason of failure to pay any poll tax or other tax. The Congress shall have power to enforce this article by appropriate legislation."[5]

Essentially, this amendment was created in order to get rid of poll taxes. These taxes were primarily used in the southern states. In order to be allowed to cast a vote, people had to pay a fee first. For many blacks, as well as poor white citizens, this fee was enough to make voting virtually impossible.[6] Poll taxes were also used along with literacy tests. With these tests, people were required to read documents aloud to prove that they could read. Some southern states skewed the tests by using very complex and difficult reading samples.[7]

Three years later, the 25th Amendment was passed. It centered on what should be done if the U.S. president is removed from office, dies, resigns, or becomes disabled. This new rule made it abundantly clear that in any of these incidents, the country's vice president takes office.[8]

Responding to Protest

If you have studied American history or listened to parents or grandparents who have talked about the 1960s and 1970s, you probably know it was a time of great national change. Young people were protesting a number of issues during this era. They fought for equality and justice by holding protests. One of the main issues they debated was the country's participation in the Vietnam War.

The war in Vietnam was unlike other wars the country had fought before. It was not a war in which America was being threatened. Instead, the nation had stepped in to help others who were under attack. Americans were strongly divided in their opinions about it. Some thought getting involved was a compassionate decision. Others thought it was a drastic mistake that was costing the lives of many U.S. soldiers.

During the early 1970s, eighteen-year-old young men were being drafted and sent to war. Those still at home, however, could not vote for or against it since the minimum voting age was twenty one years. This struck many people as unfair. If a young person was mature enough to

Two army medics try to carry a wounded paratrooper to safety while being shot at by a sniper in Vietnam, 1965.

This era of history is known for how politically involved young people were. Marching to lower the voting age was one of the many issues they participated in.

fight in a war, he should also be allowed to express political opinions about that war. The slogan some people used was, "Old enough to fight, old enough to vote."[9] Students held demonstrations protesting this unfair law. Because of the demonstrations and unrest that resulted, the 26th Amendment was adopted in summer 1971, lowering the voting age.[10]

The last amendment (thus far) was added to the Constitution in 1992.[11] An amazing fact about this amendment is that it was proposed in 1789.[12] That means it took over 200 years to be adopted. When an amendment is sent out for the ratification process, Congress determines how long it should take. The most common time period is seven years. Clearly, the 27th Amendment took far longer than that.

Simply put, the amendment states,

"No law, varying the compensation for the services of the Senators and Representatives, shall take effect, until an election of Representatives shall have intervened."[13]

This means that the salary of Congress members cannot be changed (either up or down) until the next set of terms starts. The amendment is in place to make sure that Congress cannot set its own salary, since that could easily create a conflict of interest. The amendment was sent out for ratification, but it took more than 200 years to get the necessary number of states to agree to it.

Future Amendments?

Will more Constitutional amendments be adopted in the future? Chances are very good that they will, if our history is any determination. One possibility is an amendment to force Congress to balance the national budget. This was almost passed in 1995 and may come back again soon.[14] Another possible amendment is a same-sex marriage rule. As of 2012, nine states accepted same-sex marriage, and some believe it may become a federal issue.[15]

The U.S. Constitution is one of the most amazing documents in America's history. It took immense work, time, skill, effort, and discussion on the part of wise men to determine what would be included in it. The document was important then—and still is today. However, it was not perfect then and it isn't today. As time passes, issues change and so amendments were made to keep this "living document" updated and relevant.

The weight of responsibility similar to what Lincoln felt long ago is one that modern presidents and other government officials continue to endure when faced with making Constitutional decisions. It is not easy to consider the well-being of millions of people all at once, and the amendment process is slow but thorough for that reason. It protects America's people—yesterday, today, and tomorrow.

Failed Amendments

Most proposed amendments fail, but they are interesting to learn about anyway. Some failed amendments include

- Renaming the United States the "United States of the Earth" (1893)
- Acknowledging that the Constitution recognizes God and Jesus Christ as the supreme authorities in human affairs (1894)
- Making marriage between races illegal (1912)
- Making divorce illegal (1914)
- Putting any acts of war to a national vote (1916)
- Limiting personal wealth to $1 million (1933)
- Forbidding drunkenness throughout the country (1938)
- Making flag desecration illegal (1968–2006)
- Allowing prayer in school (2003)[16]

New amendments are sure to be added in years to come.

Years of Ratification

1776 U.S. Constitution

1791 Bill of Rights

1795 11th Amendment

1804 12th Amendment

1865 13th Amendment

1868 14th and 15th Amendments

1913 16th and 17th Amendments

1919 18th Amendment

1920 19th Amendment

1933 20th and 21st Amendments

1951 22nd Amendment

1961 23rd Amendment

1964 24th Amendment

1967 25th Amendment

1971 26th Amendment

1992 27th Amendment

CHAPTER NOTES

Chapter 1

1. Chief Justice Charles Evans Hughes, "The Republic Endures and This is the Symbol of its Faith," Supreme Court of the United States. http://www.supremecourt.gov/about/constitutional.aspx
2. Glenn Whipp, "Oscars 2013: Daniel Day-Lewis wins best actor for *Lincoln*," *Los Angeles Times*, February 24, 2013.

Chapter 2

1. U.S. HIstory Online Textbook, "Antifederalists," US.history.org, http://www.ushistory.org/us/16b.asp
2. U.S. History Online Textbook, "Federalists," US.history.org, http://www.ushistory.org/us/16a.asp
3. Robert Longley, "The Original Bill of Rights had 12 Amendments," About.com U.S. Government Info, December 13, 2010. http://usgovinfo.about.com/od/usconstitution/a/The-Original-Bill-Of-Rights-Had-12-Amendments.htm
4. "The Bill of Rights is Finally Ratified," History.com, http://www.history.com/this-day-in-history/bill-of-rights-is-finally-ratified
5. Ibid.
6. United States Constitution, http://constitutionus.com/
7. Celebrate the Constitution, "Bill of Rights," *Scholastic,* http://teacher.scholastic.com/scholasticnews/indepth/constitution_day/background/index.asp?article=billofrights

Chapter 3

1. "States ratify 11th amendment, limiting power of federal courts." Centuries of Citizenship: A Constitutional Timeline, National Constitution Center, http://constitutioncenter.org/timeline/html/cw03_11967.html
2. Ibid.
3. "Background of the Twelfth Amendment," United States History, http://www.u-s-history.com/pages/h468.html
4. James R. Whitson, "The Electoral Process before the 12th Amendment," President Elect, May 2000, http://presidentelect.org/art_before12.html
5. United States Constitution, http://constitutionus.com/
6. Abraham Lincoln, "House Divided," Oregon Public Broadcasting, Supreme Court History: The First Hundred Years, http://www.pbs.org/wnet/supremecourt/antebellum/sources_document13.html
7. "13th Amendment to the U.S. Constitution: Abolition of Slavery (1865)," Our Documents, http://www.ourdocuments.gov/doc.php?flash=true&doc=40
8. "The Civil War and Emancipation," Oregon Public Broadcasting, Africans in America: Judgment Day, http://www.pbs.org/wgbh/aia/part4/4p2967.html
9. "Dred Scott v. Sandford (1857)," Oregon Public Broadcasting, Supreme Court History: The First Hundred Years, http://www.pbs.org/wnet/supremecourt/antebellum/landmark_dred.html
10. United States Constitution, http://constitutionus.com/
11. "Abolitionist," National Susan B. Anthony Museum and House, http://susanbanthonyhouse.org/her-story/abolitionist.php
12. Ibid.

Chapter 4

1. "16th Amendment," Laws.com, http://kids.laws.com/16th-amendment
2. United States Constitution, http://constitutionus.com/
3. "17th Amendment to the U.S. Constitution: Direct Election of U.S. Senators," OurDocuments.gov, http://www.ourdocuments.gov/doc.php?flash=true&doc=58
4. Ibid.
5. "The Temperance Movement," United States History, http://www.u-s-history.com/pages/h1054.html
6. "Prohibition of Alcohol," Nebraska Studies.org, http://www.nebraskastudies.org/0700/frameset_reset.html?http://www.nebraskastudies.org/0700/stories/0701_0125.html
7. "Unintended Consequences," Prohibition, PBS.org, http://www.pbs.org/kenburns/prohibition/unintended-consequences/
8. Ibid.
9. "Organized Crime and Prohibition," http://www.albany.edu/~wm731882/organized_crime1_final.html

10. "Unintended Consequences," Prohibition, PBS.org, http://www.pbs.org/kenburns/prohibition/unintended-consequences/

11. Geoff Tibbals, *The Mammoth Book of Zingers, Quips, and One-Liners* (New York: Caroll & Graf, 2005), p. 178.

12. "Women's Fight for the Vote: The Nineteenth Amendment," Exploring Constitutional Conflicts, http://law2.umkc.edu/faculty/projects/ftrials/conlaw/nineteentham.htm

13. United States Constitution, http://constitutionus.com/

14. "The Constitution and the Inauguration of the President," Exploring Constitutional Law, http://law2.umkc.edu/faculty/projects/ftrials/conlaw/inaugurationconstit.html

15. Twenty-First Amendment, Free Dictionary.com, http://legal-dictionary.thefreedictionary.com/21st+Amendment

16. "Proposed Amendments," Constitution Facts, http://www.constitutionfacts.com/?section=constitution&page=proposedAmendments.cfm

Chapter 5

1. "Twenty-Second Amendment to the United States Constitution," The Free Dictionary, http://encyclopedia.thefreedictionary.com/22nd+Amendment+to+the+United+States+Constitution

2. "How many presidents served more than one term as president?" Wisegeek.com, http://www.wisegeek.com/how-many-us-presidents-served-more-than-one-term-as-president.htm

3. Ibid.

4. "Twenty-third Amendment to the United States Constitution," The Free Dictionary, http://encyclopedia.thefreedictionary.com/23rd+Amendment+to+the+United+States+Constitution

5. United States Constitution, http://constitutionus.com/

6. "The 24th Amendment Ended the Poll Tax," America's Story, The Library of Congress, http://www.americaslibrary.gov/jb/modern/jb_modern_polltax_1.html

7. Literacy Tests, NAACP: A Century in the Fight for Freedom, Library of Congress, http://myloc.gov/Exhibitions/naacp/civilrightsera/ExhibitObjects/LiteracyTests.aspx

8. "Twenty-fifth Amendment to the United States Constitution," The Free Dictionary, http://encyclopedia.thefreedictionary.com/25th+Amendment+to+the+United+States+Constitution

9. "The 26th Amendment," History Channel, http://www.history.com/topics/the-26th-amendment

10. "Twenty-fifth Amendment to the United States Constitution," The Free Dictionary, http://encyclopedia.thefreedictionary.com/25th+Amendment+to+the+United+States+Constitution

11. "Twenty-seventh Amendment to the United States Constitution," The Free Dictionary, http://encyclopedia.thefreedictionary.com/27th+Amendment+to+the+United+States+Constitution

12. Ibid.

13. United States Constitution, http://constitutionus.com/

14. "House Rejects Balanced Budget Amendment," *USA Today,* November 18, 2011, http://usatoday30.usatoday.com/news/washington/story/2011-11-18/balanced-budget-amendment-house-vote/51297960/1

15. "Defining Marriage: Defense of Marriage Acts and Same-Sex Marriage Laws," National Conference of State Legislatures, November 2012, http://www.ncsl.org/issues-research/human-services/same-sex-marriage-overview.aspx

16. "Proposed Amendments," Clayton State University, 2012, http://www.clayton.edu/arts-sciences/constitutionday/proposedamendments

Books

Burgan, Michael. *The Reconstruction Amendments.* North Mankato, MN: Compass Point Books, 2006.

Orr, Tamra. *The Tenth Amendment: Limiting Federal Power.* New York: Rosen Books, 2012.

Smith, Rich. *How Amendments are Adopted.* Minneapolis, MN: Abdo Publishing, 2007.

Sobel, Syl. *The Bill of Rights: Protecting Our Freedom Then and Now.* New York: Barron's Educational Series, 2008.

Stange, Mark. *Understanding the U.S. Constitution.* Greensboro, NC: Mark Twain Media, 2008.

Travis, Cathy. *Constitution Translated for Kids.* Dallas, TX: Ovation Books, 2008.

Turner, Juliette. *Our Constitution Rocks!* Grand Rapids, MI: Zondervan Books, 2012.

Works Consulted

Bomboy, Scott. "What will be the next constitutional amendment?" *Constitution Daily.* July 30, 2012. http://blog.constitutioncenter. org/2012/07/what-will-be-the-next-constitutional-amendment/

Celebrate the Constitution, "Bill of Rights." *Scholastic.* No date. http://teacher. scholastic.com/scholasticnews/indepth/constitution_day/background/ index.asp?article=billofrights

Remy, Richard C. *U.S. Government: Democracy in Action.* Glencoe: Ohio, 2006.

Travis, Cathy. *Constitution Translated for Kids.* Ovation Books: Texas, 2008.

Whipp, Glenn. "Oscars 2013: Daniel Day-Lewis wins best actor for *Lincoln.*" *Los Angeles Times*, February 24, 2013.

On the Internet

Bill of Rights Institute
    http://billofrightsinstitute.org/
The Charters of Freedom
    http://www.archives.gov/exhibits/charters/bill_of_rights.html
Cornell University Law School
    http://www.law.cornell.edu/constitution/billofrights

abolish—Formally put an end to (a system, practice, or institution).

amend—Make minor changes to a document in order to make it more accurate, or more up-to-date, or to modify it formally, as a legal document or legislative bill.

Anti-Federalist—One who opposes a federal government—applied particularly to the party which opposed the adoption of the Constitution of the United States.

assassinate—To murder (an important person) in a surprise attack for political or religious reasons.

atheist—A person who denies or disbelieves the existence of a supreme being.

bail—The temporary release of an accused person awaiting trial, sometimes on the condition that a sum of money be lodged to guarantee their appearance in court.

censor—To examine material (books, movies, documents, etc.) and suppress parts that are considered inappropriate.

civil suit—A lawsuit alleging violations of civil (as opposed to criminal) law.

convention—An official gathering of members to vote, or for another official purpose.

descendant—A person who comes from a particular ancestor through birth (i.e. child, grandchild).

Electoral College—A body of people representing the states of the United States who formally cast votes for the election of the president and vice president.

Federalist—An advocate or supporter of federalism and the Constitution.

libel—A published, false statement that damages a person's reputation.

liberties—Freedoms or rights.

literacy—The ability to read and write.

poll tax—A tax levied on people in order to vote in elections.

Prohibition—A period of time when alcohol was illegal to buy, sell, or transport.

ratify—To sign or give formal consent to make something officially valid.

reconstruction—Rebuilding something that has been damaged or destroyed.

repeal—To revoke a law or congressional act.

representative—A person chosen or appointed to act or speak for a group of people.

slander—Making a spoken, false statement that damages a person's reputation.

temperance—Abstinence from alcohol consumption.

tyrannical—Oppressive and controlling.

warrant—A document issued by a legal or government official authorizing police or another body to make an arrest or search.

INDEX

Tamra Orr is author of more than 350 nonfiction books for readers of all ages. She has written a number of historical books, including *The Story of the Constitution*, *The People at the Center of Prohibition*, *The Biography of Susan B. Anthony*, and *The Tenth Amendment*, plus many books about celebrities, foreign countries, and health and medical conditions. Orr is a graduate of Ball State University in Muncie, Indiana. In 2001, she and her family moved from Indiana to Oregon. She is mother to four, and a homeschooler. Orr loves to read, write letters, go camping, and travel throughout the country.